BIOLOGY Field Notes

Be a MANTA RAY Expert

by
E. C. Andrews

Minneapolis, Minnesota

Credits
All images are courtesy of Shutterstock.com, unless otherwise specified. With thanks to Getty Images, Thinkstock Photo, and iStockphoto.

Recurring – LadadikArt, Milano M, The_Pixel, yana shypova, Baksiabat, vectorplus, Anna Frajtova, Wahyuwm48, NotionPic. Character throughout – NotionPic. Cover – Vladimir Turkenich, The_Pixel, Milano M, Baksiabat, vectorplus, Anna Frajtova, Wahyuwm48, Wonderful Nature. 4–5 – Kjersti Joergensen, Michael Bogner. 6–7 – Aaronejbull87, Wirestock Creators. 8–9 – David Keep, Choksawatdikorn, Dan Tilert, Philip Thurston. 10–11 – blxckdiamond, chonlasub woravichan. 12–13 – Dudarev Mikhail, nicolasvoisin44. 14–15 – wildestanimal, Sadie Whitelocks. 16–17 – wildestanimal. 18–19 – Lewis Burnett, Kjersti Joergensen. 20–21 – Aaronejbull87, sergemi. 22–23 – Aaronejbull87, Denis Moskvinov.

Bearport Publishing Company Product Development Team
Publisher: Jen Jenson; Director of Product Development: Spencer Brinker; Managing Editor: Allison Juda; Editor: Cole Nelson; Associate Editor: Naomi Reich; Associate Editor: Tiana Tran; Designer: Kim Jones; Designer: Kayla Eggert; Designer: Steve Scheluchin; Production Specialist: Owen Hamlin

Library of Congress Cataloging-in-Publication Data is available at www.loc.gov or upon request from the publisher.

ISBN: 979-8-89577-006-1 (hardcover)
ISBN: 979-8-89577-437-3 (paperback)
ISBN: 979-8-89577-123-5 (ebook)

© 2026 BookLife Publishing
This edition is published by arrangement with BookLife Publishing.

North American adaptations © 2026 Bearport Publishing Company. All rights reserved. No part of this publication may be reproduced in whole or in part, stored in any retrieval system, or transmitted in any form or by any means, electronic, mechanical, photocopying, recording, or otherwise, without written permission from thepublisher. Bearport Publishing is a division of FlutterBee Education Group.

For more information, write to Bearport Publishing, 5357 Penn Avenue South, Minneapolis, MN 55419.

CONTENTS

Meet the Biologist............4
A Manta Ray's Body..........6
Underwater Homes...........8
A Squadron..................10
Dinner Time.................12
Mysterious Migrations......16
Jumping for Joy............18
Life Cycle...................20
Magnificent Manta Rays....22
Glossary....................24
Index.......................24

A MANTA RAY'S BODY

Manta rays are named after their wide, flat bodies. In Spanish, the word *manta* means blanket or cloak. These creatures look like floating blankets or as if they are wearing cloaks.

There are more than 600 kinds of rays. Manta rays are the largest in the world.

On the sides of a manta ray's head are two fins called cephalic lobes (suh-FAH-lik lowbz). Manta rays use these fins to catch food and to **communicate** with other mantas.

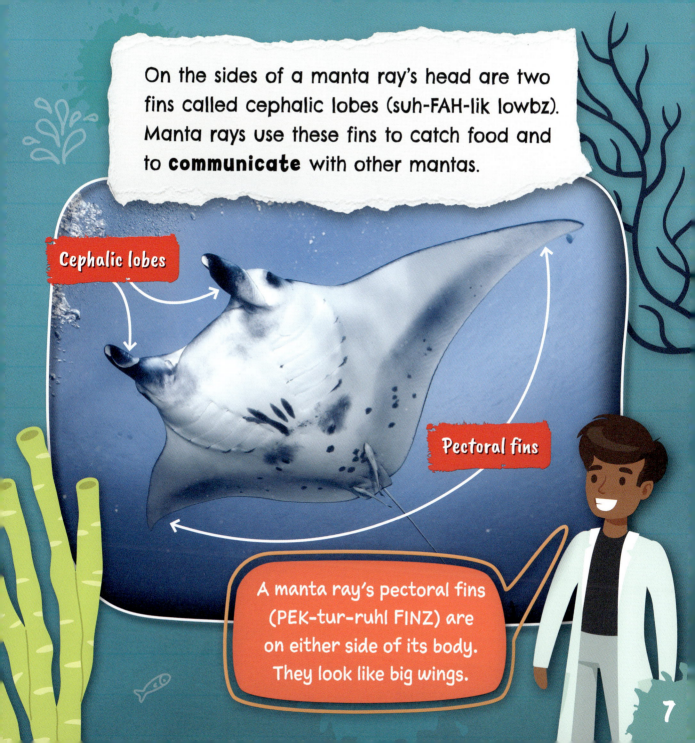

Cephalic lobes

Pectoral fins

A manta ray's pectoral fins (PEK-tur-ruhl FINZ) are on either side of its body. They look like big wings.

UNDERWATER HOMES

Manta rays are found in **tropical** to **temperate** bodies of water around the world. Like most fish, mantas do not breathe air. They can only breathe underwater.

A giant oceanic manta ray

The two types of manta rays are giant oceanic mantas and reef mantas.

A coral reef

A reef manta

For mantas, having an open ocean to swim in is important. Giant oceanic mantas often hunt in deep water. Reef mantas tend to stay in shallow waters near the shore.

Both open oceans and coral reefs are manta ray **habitats.**

A SQUADRON

Manta rays may live alone or in small groups. Those that live together help one another hunt **prey**. Mantas also meet up every two to five years to **mate**.

A group of mantas is called a squadron.

Another reason mantas may come together is to clean their bodies. They often meet at cleaning stations, which are places with lots of tiny fish. These fish eat the **parasites** found on the manta rays' bodies.

A cleaning station

Cleaning stations keep manta rays healthy and help small fish get food.

DINNER TIME

How do manta rays feed? They open their big mouths! Inside, there are rows of tiny rakes called gill plates. These are used to trap prey as water goes past them.

Gill plates

Manta rays close their mouths when they are not feeding.

First, manta rays swim with their mouths open to take in prey. Then, they swallow their meal and spit out the extra water. This is called filter feeding. Manta rays can swallow only small creatures, such as krill and zooplankton.

A zooplankton

Zooplankton are tiny creatures that float around in the ocean.

Manta rays do more than just swim in straight lines with their mouths open. They can sometimes get very creative during hunts! Manta rays may do underwater somersaults to catch as much prey as they can.

Manta mealtimes can be fun to watch.

A manta somersaulting

Manta rays have a clever way of hunting in groups. The squadron swims in circles to surround the prey. This trick is called cyclone feeding. It prevents the food from escaping.

When more than 100 mantas swim in circles, it's called a manta ray whirlwind!

MYSTERIOUS MIGRATIONS

Manta rays go wherever there is warm water and plenty to eat. Some squadrons gather to travel long distances together to find a better feeding place. This is called a migration.

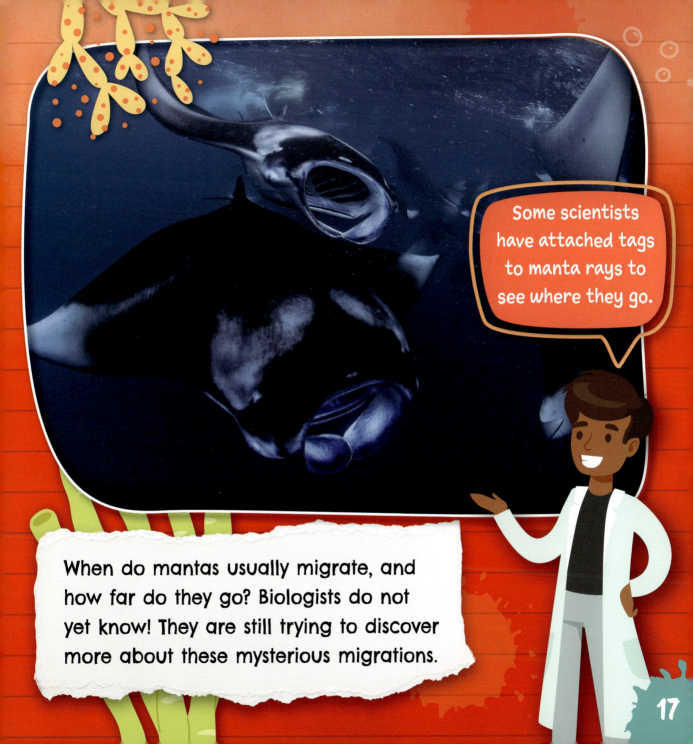

JUMPING FOR JOY

Manta rays can often be seen leaping out of the water. This is called breaching. Biologists are not sure why manta rays breach, but they have a few ideas.

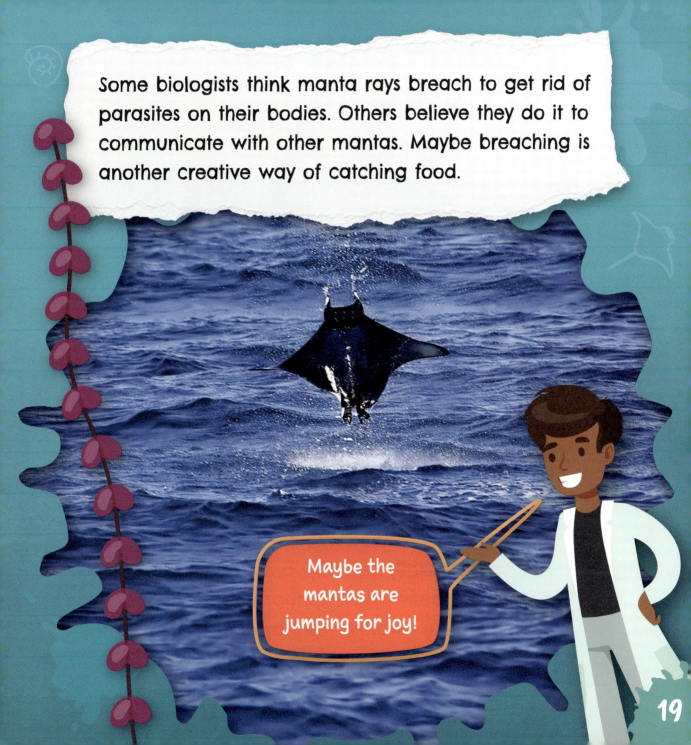

Some biologists think manta rays breach to get rid of parasites on their bodies. Others believe they do it to communicate with other mantas. Maybe breaching is another creative way of catching food.

Maybe the mantas are jumping for joy!

LIFE CYCLE

Manta rays are ovoviviparous (OH-vo-vye-VI-puh-ruhs), which means manta babies **hatch** from eggs while still inside their mothers. After about 13 months, the little rays come out with their pectoral fins wrapped around themselves, almost like a burrito!

Baby manta rays are called pups.

As soon as a baby manta is born, it leaves its mother's care. When it is about 10 years old, a manta ray is ready to find a mate and have pups of its own. Manta rays usually have one or two pups every few years.

Manta rays can live for about 50 years.

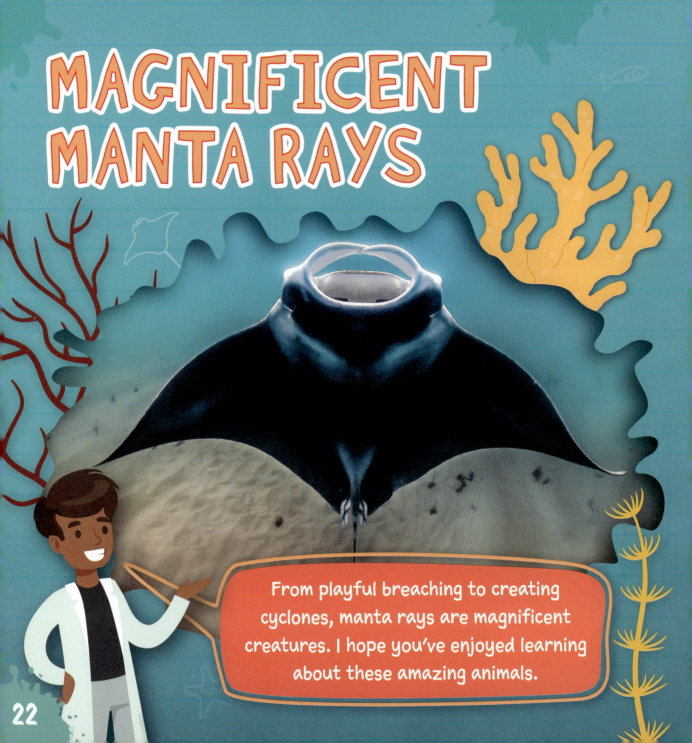

MAGNIFICENT MANTA RAYS

From playful breaching to creating cyclones, manta rays are magnificent creatures. I hope you've enjoyed learning about these amazing animals.

GLOSSARY

biologist a person who studies and knows a lot about living things

communicate to share information

expert a person who knows a lot about something

habitats places in nature where animals normally live

hatch when a manta ray breaks out of its egg

mate to come together to have young

parasites living things that get food by living on or in other plants or animals

prey animals that are hunted and eaten by other animals

temperate having a climate with different seasons and few weather extremes compared to hot or cold areas

tropical a hot and humid region

INDEX

bodies 6–8, 11, 19
cyclones 15, 22
fins 7, 20
fish 4, 8, 11, 16
food 7, 19
migrate 16–17
oceans 4, 9, 13
parasites 11, 19
pups 20–21
reefs 8–9
water 8–9, 12–13, 16, 18, 22